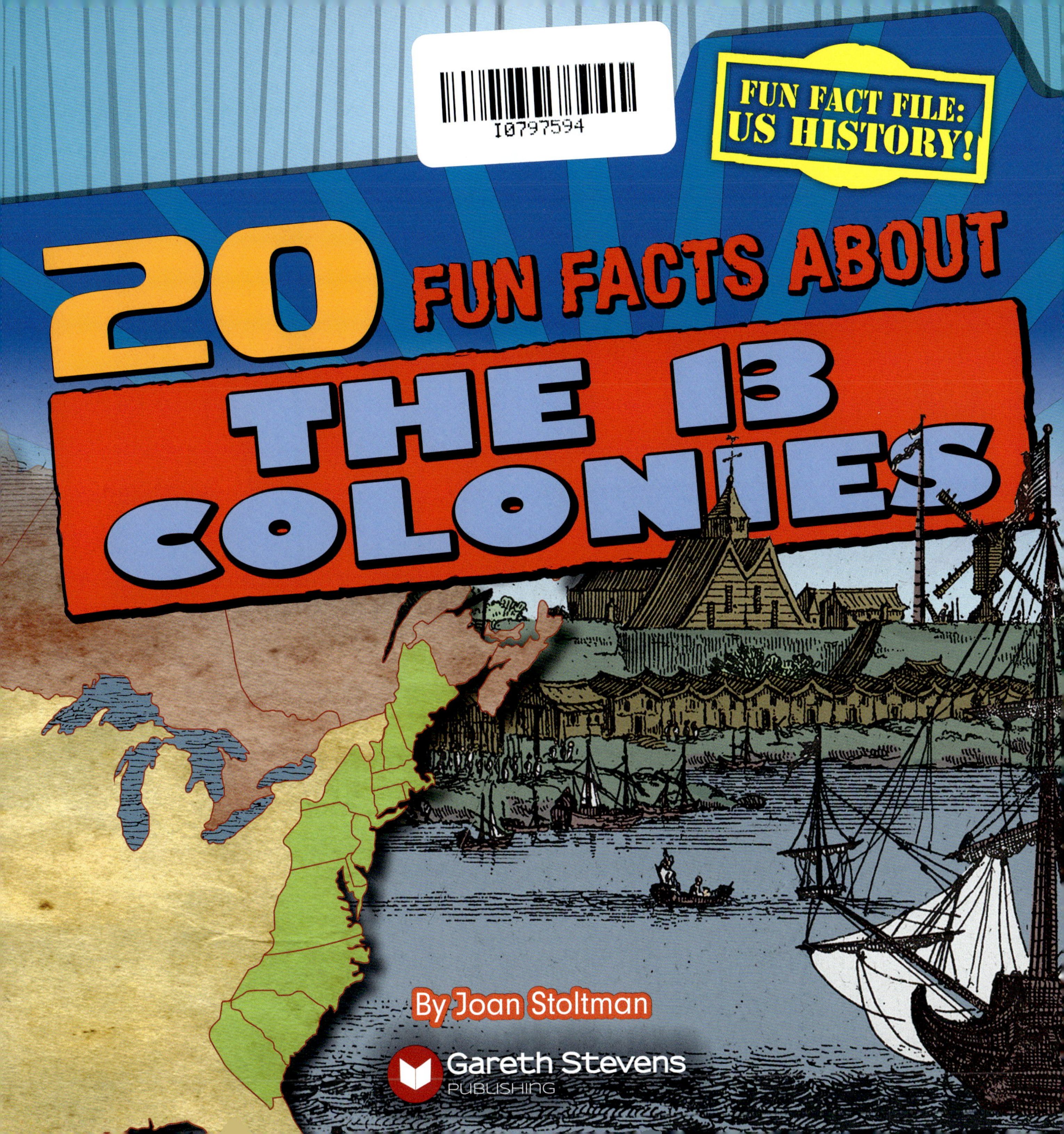
I0797594
FUN FACT FILE: US HISTORY!
20 FUN FACTS ABOUT THE 13 COLONIES
By Joan Stoltman
Gareth Stevens
PUBLISHING

Please visit our website, www.garethstevens.com. For a free color catalog of all our high-quality books, call toll free 1-800-542-2595 or fax 1-877-542-2596.

Library of Congress Cataloging-in-Publication Data

Names: Stoltman, Joan, author.
Title: 20 fun facts about the 13 colonies / Joan Stoltman.
Description: New York : Gareth Stevens Publishing, 2019. | Series: Fun fact files: US history! | Includes index.
Identifiers: LCCN 2017060748| ISBN 9781538219058 (library bound) | ISBN 9781538219034 (pbk.) | ISBN 9781538219041 (6 pack)
Subjects: LCSH: United States–History–Colonial period, ca. 1600-1775–Juvenile literature.
Classification: LCC E188 .S87 2018 | DDC 973.2–dc23
LC record available at https://lccn.loc.gov/2017060748

Published in 2019 by
Gareth Stevens Publishing
111 East 14th Street, Suite 349
New York, NY 10003

Designer: Sarah Liddell
Editor: Mariel Bard

Photo credits: Cover, p. 1 (map) Ad_hominem/Shutterstock.com; cover, p. 1 (image) De Agostini Picture Library/Contributor/De Agostini/Getty Images; p. 5 Cg-realms/Wikimedia Commons; p. 6 Ealdgyth/Wikimedia Commons; p. 7 Everett Historical/Shutterstock.com; p. 8 OgreBot/Wikimedia Commons; p. 9 Jan Arkesteijn/Wikimedia Commons; pp. 10, 14 Bettmann/Contributor/Bettmann/Getty Images; p. 11 Magicpiano/Wikimedia Commons; p. 12 Grendelkhan/Wikimedia Commons; pp. 13, 26 (George Washington) Scewing/Wikimedia Commons; p. 15 Education Images/Contributor/Universal Images Group/Getty Images; p. 16 William Maury Morris II/Wikimedia Commons; pp. 17, 24 MarmadukePercy/Wikimedia Commons; pp. 18, 22 Joseph Sohm/Shutterstock.com; p. 19 DEA/VENERANDA BIBLIOTECA AMBROSIANA/Contributor/De Agostini/Getty Images; p. 20 (apothecary) Chamille White/Shutterstock.com; p. 20 (blacksmith) Noska Photo/Shutterstock.com; p. 20 (cooper) B Brown/Shutterstock.com; p. 21 (chandler) aleks333/Shutterstock.com; p. 21 (cobbler) Ritu Manoj Jethani/Shutterstock.com; p. 21 (wheelwright) JFs Pic S. Thielemann/Shutterstock.com; p. 23 Raydu18/Wikimedia Commons; p. 25 Gallop/Wikimedia Commons; p. 26 (James Madison) Botaurus/Wikimedia Commons; p. 26 (James Monroe) Maximilian Schönherr/Wikimedia Commons; p. 26 (Thomas Jefferson) Clindberg/Wikimedia Commons; p. 27 Makaristos/Wikimedia Commons; p. 29 Michael Gordon/Shutterstock.com.

Printed in the United States of America

CPSIA compliance information: Batch #CS18GS: For further information contact Gareth Stevens, New York, New York at 1-800-542-2595.

Contents

Words in the glossary appear in **bold** type the first time they are used in the text.

Before the States United

In 1587, the first British settlers arrived in what would become the United States of America. For about 200 years, settlers came and built up colonies. A colony is an area under the control of another country that's usually far away. The British had control of 13 colonies along the Atlantic coast. Other European countries had some land in North America in its earliest colonial days, too, and many Native Americans had been living there for hundreds of years already.

Most colonists worked on farms, making goods that weren't found in England. The British used these goods to make money off the colonies.

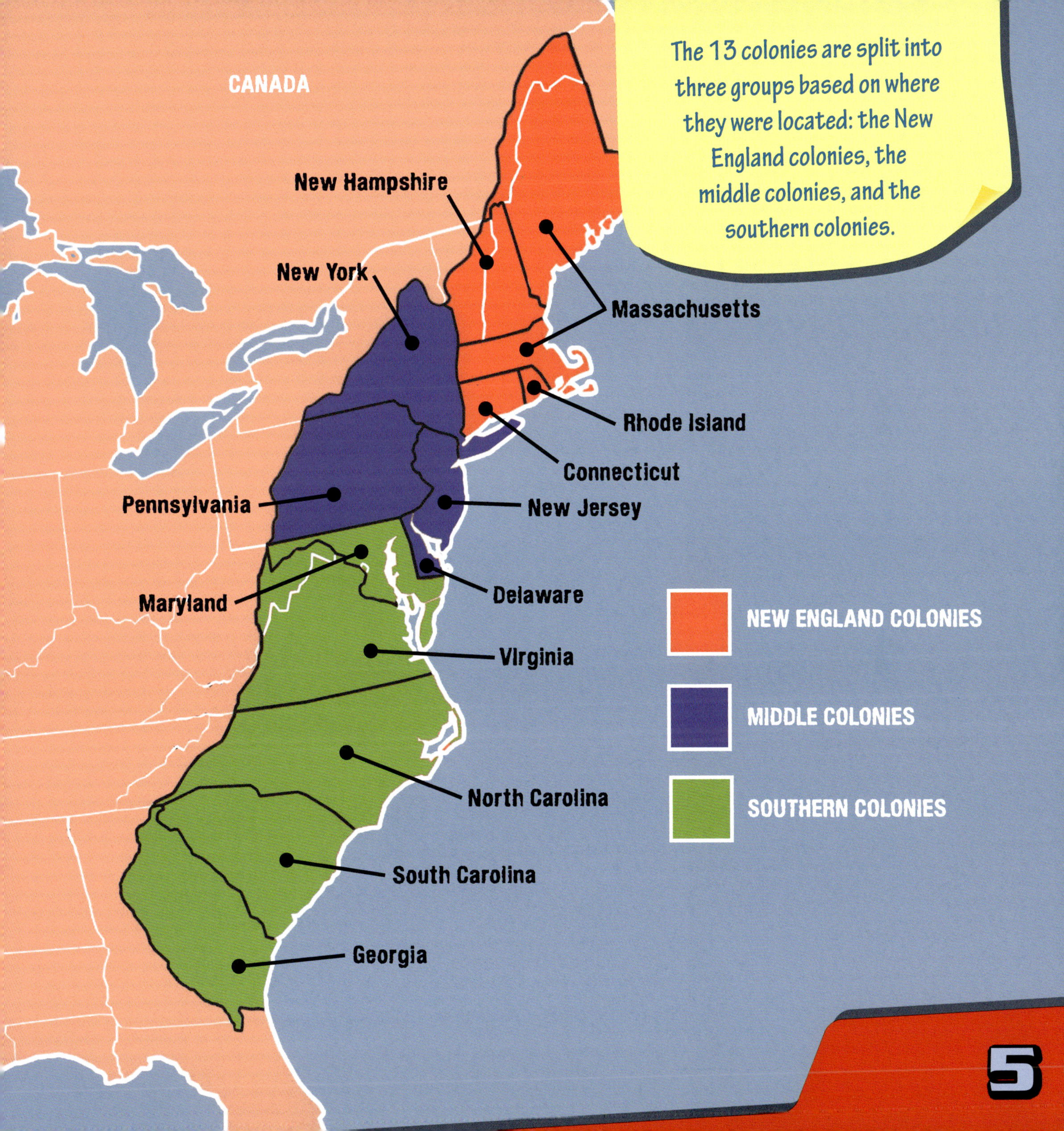

The 13 colonies are split into three groups based on where they were located: the New England colonies, the middle colonies, and the southern colonies.

Founding Facts

FACT 1

Plymouth Colony wasn't one of the 13 colonies!

Plymouth Colony was the first permanent, or long-lasting, British settlement in New England. The Pilgrims founded it in 1620, seeking freedom of **religion** and an easier life. In 1691, Plymouth became part of the Massachusetts Bay Colony.

Mayflower

The Pilgrims left England in September 1620. They sailed across the Atlantic Ocean on the *Mayflower* for 2 months before they reached Massachusetts.

Maryland and Rhode Island were founded as places for religious freedom.

Roger Williams

Puritans were a group of people in the colonies who believed laws should be based on the Bible. In Rhode Island, though, people wanted to keep religion out of government. This practice is called the separation of church and state.

Maryland was settled in 1634 by Cecil Calvert as a safe place for people of the Catholic faith. Rhode Island was settled in 1636 by Roger Williams.

FACT 3

The colony of Connecticut was founded over a disagreement between two Puritan leaders!

Thomas Hooker didn't like how John Cotton was running Boston, Massachusetts. So, in 1636, Hooker and his followers walked south to find land for a new colony—Connecticut!

Hooker and his followers leaving Massachusetts

Hooker thought people should be able to vote no matter what their religious beliefs were. This became an important part of American government.

The colony of Pennsylvania was founded because King Charles II owed someone money!

In 1681, the king of England gave William Penn more than 45,000 square miles (117,000 square km) of land because he owed Penn's father a lot of money. This land became the colony of Pennsylvania.

William Penn didn't earn much from the Pennsylvania Colony. He died in 1718 with no money.

FACT 5

Slavery wasn't allowed in Georgia when the colony was founded.

James Oglethorpe founded the colony of Georgia in 1732 with many rules. But after Oglethorpe returned to England in 1743, the colonists stopped following his rules! The number of slaves in Georgia soon boomed.

As Georgia's first governor, Oglethorpe also banned rum, which is a type of **alcohol**. This rule was broken, too!

Native American Lands

William Penn paid Native Americans in farm tools, cooking tools, weapons, and clothes.

Some colonial leaders believed in treating Native Americans fairly. But many colonists didn't agree. They pushed Native Americans off the land the groups had lived on for many years. Fighting over land was common.

Very often, Native American groups weren't paid anything for the land the colonists took.

FACT 7

Colonists in Windham, Connecticut, once thought they were being attacked by Native Americans—but it was just frogs!

Terrible noises surrounded the town one night in 1754. Some people went to look around and fight back, but they found nothing. The next morning, they realized the noises had been made by frogs!

frog statue near Windham, Connecticut

Colonists were often afraid of attack at this time. The British and French were at war in North America and many Native American groups had taken sides.

FACT 8

The Salem witch trials were started by children.

In 1692, Betty Parris, age 9, and Abigail Williams, age 11, accused, or blamed, three women of being witches. The trials lasted about a year. Over 200 people were accused and 20 were killed.

Puritan churches held witch trials throughout Massachusetts Bay Colony, not just in Salem. The trials were ruled unlawful in 1702.

Colonial children were put to work at a very young age.

Children who lived on farms had little, if any, education. Boys would help their father, and girls would help their mother. Both boys and girls learned skills they could use later in life.

Colonial boys often learned to read and write from their father or at church—but girls weren't usually taught how.

George Washington made and sold a type of alcohol called whiskey.

FACT 10

In colonial times, everyone—even kids—drank beer, a type of alcoholic drink!

Water often made people ill because it wasn't clean. Instead, colonists drank beer, cider, and tea made with boiled water. In New England, colonists grew lots of apples to make hard cider, which is another type of alcohol.

Colonial widows and unmarried women had more rights than married women!

Widows and unmarried women could sign contracts, make **wills**, and buy and sell land. Some widows never remarried because they liked this independence so much.

Sometimes, a widow took over her husband's business after he died.

FACT 12

The population of the colonies exploded between 1700 and 1770.

In 1700, when there were only 12 colonies (Georgia joined in 1732), the colonies had 260,000 people. By 1770, there were over 2 million people! Settlers continued to come from Europe as the colonies grew.

People in the colonies used trenchers, or plates made of wood. They also ate with their hands much of the time.

FACT 13

Some colonial children stood around the table during meals.

Poorer families often didn't own enough chairs for everyone in the house—which isn't surprising with such large families!

Many farm animals in the colonies were brought over from Europe!

Domesticated cows, sheep, and pigs aren't native to North America. Just like the people who came to the colonies, many animals were also brought by ship.

Large animals weren't brought over on the *Mayflower*. Colonists had to wait a few years for the first cows and sheep to arrive.

Jobs in Colonial Times

APOTHECARY
made and sold **medicines**; sometimes acted as a doctor

TAVERN OWNER
ran a meeting place that sold food and drinks

BLACKSMITH
made and fixed iron items such as tools and nails

COOPER
made **containers** for storing items such as beer, wine, flour, and gunpowder

TAILOR
made clothing from cloth people would bring in, which was often bought from the milliner

GUNSMITH
fixed guns using wood and metal; sometimes made new guns

People had all kinds of jobs in colonial times. Many of these jobs don't exist today!

COBBLER
made and fixed shoes

WHEELWRIGHT
made and fixed wagon wheels using wood and iron

WIGMAKER
made wigs for rich men; also shaved men's faces and styled hair

CABINETMAKER
made furniture, such as desks, chairs, and tables, for the rich

CHANDLER
made candles

MILLINER
sold cloth, thread, hats, shirts, and more; one of the few jobs women could work

Home, Sweet Home

FACT 15

Early colonial farmers' homes had dirt floors and only a few rooms.

These homes had wood frames filled in with sticks called "wattle." Spaces between the sticks were filled in with "daub," a sticky matter made from grass, clay, and mud.

"Wattle and daub" houses usually had thatched roofs, which were made from dried grasses. A grass roof meant house fires were often impossible to stop!

Plantation homes had many rooms and were filled with expensive furniture. Thomas Jefferson, the third president, lived on this grand plantation called Monticello.

FACT 16

Plantation houses were big, fancy, and expensive.

Certain crops, such as cotton and **tobacco**, grew better in the warmer weather of the southern colonies. Plantation owners became rich off these crops and built big homes with huge porches and tall windows.

FACT 17

In 1687, colonists stuck official government papers in a tree to hide them from a governor!

The governor was Sir Edmund Andros, and he needed Connecticut's **charter** if he wanted to take over the colony. The colonists didn't want that, so they hid the charter so he couldn't find it!

The tree became known as the "Charter Oak."

This is an artist's take on the Battles of Saratoga, which took place in Stillwater, New York, in 1777.

FACT 18

Almost one-third of the American Revolution was fought in what is now New York State!

The turning point of the war came when the American colonists beat the British in the Battles of Saratoga. It showed that the colonists could fight—and win—on their own against a European army.

FACT 19

Virginia Colony was home to four of the first five American presidents!

George Washington, Thomas Jefferson, James Madison, and James Monroe were all from there. John Adams, the second president, was from Massachusetts.

It's no wonder so many early presidents came from Virginia Colony—it was huge!

This is one of the first of many flags the United States has had over the years.

FACT 20

The symbols of the flag have special meaning.

In 1777, the Second Continental Congress decided the official flag for the new United States of America should have 13 stripes to show the importance of the 13 colonies. Stars have been added to the flag each time the United States gained a state, but the 13 stripes have never changed!

More, More, More!

There are so many more fun facts about the colonies. For example, did you know there was an earlier colony called Roanoke on an island off the coast of North Carolina? It was founded in 1587, but by 1590, the colonists had all vanished! What happened to them is still a mystery.

Today, you can visit outdoor museums that look like colonial villages. At Plymouth Plantation in Massachusetts, you'll find a colonial village, a Native American village, and a ship like the *Mayflower*. You can also visit Colonial Williamsburg in Virgina to see what colonial life was like for yourself!

Colonial Williamsburg is a community of museums, shops, and more in Williamsburg, Virginia. It also features a historical area where everything is just like it was in the 1700s!

Glossary

alcohol: a liquid found in some drinks, such as beer and wine, that can make someone have trouble moving, talking, and thinking

American Revolution: the war in which the colonies won their freedom from England

charter: an official agreement giving permission to do something

container: an object used to hold something

domesticate: to breed and raise for people to use

medicine: a drug taken to make a sick person well

plantation: a large farm

religion: a belief in and way of honoring a god or gods

symbol: a picture, shape, or object that stands for something else

tobacco: a plant with leaves that can be smoked

trial: a formal meeting in which facts about a crime are presented to a judge

widow: a woman whose husband has died

will: a document stating the wishes of someone who has died

For More Information

Books

Fajardo, Anika. *The Dish on Food and Farming in Colonial America*. Mankato, MN: Capstone Press, 2012.

Mara, Wil. *If You Were a Kid in the Thirteen Colonies*. New York, NY: Children's Press, 2017.

Vonne, Mira. *Gross Facts About the American Colonies*. North Mankato, MN: Capstone Press, 2017.

Websites

Build Your Plantation
mdroots.thinkport.org/interactives/plantation/intro.asp
This fun online game lets you run a Maryland plantation. Play along and see if you can build, plant, and sell enough to make a living.

Colonial House: Interactive History
www.thirteen.org/kids/wnet/colonialhouse/history/index.html
Visit this interactive website for more information about the colonies.

Kid Zone
www.history.org/kids/index.cfm
Learn about Colonial Williamsburg here.

Publisher's note to educators and parents: Our editors have carefully reviewed these websites to ensure that they are suitable for students. Many websites change frequently, however, and we cannot guarantee that a site's future contents will continue to meet our high standards of quality and educational value. Be advised that students should be closely supervised whenever they access the internet.

Index